Face Everything And Rise

poems on transmuting pain into grace

the wounded healer

BookLeaf
Publishing

India | USA | UK

Made with ❤ on the BookLeaf Publishing Platform
www.bookleafpub.in
www.bookleafpub.com

Dedication

this poetry collection is a prayer, whispered in love, for every soul who has felt the ground give way beneath them—who has fallen, unbidden, into the seemingly endless abyss of pain and loss. hold fast to hope, dear traveler. fix your gaze upon the light, even when darkness is all you know. within every shadow, a seed of transformation waits to bloom.

may you have the courage to trust that Love beyond all names and forms is weaving everything together with divine intention. there is meaning in your sorrow and healing beyond what you can yet imagine.
even now, it is unfolding.

may your suffering become a doorway, leading you deeper into Love, Truth, and Faith.

may you find the courage within to find that fear and anger are teachers, not foes.

and in every wound, may you discover a window to grace.

"if you are irritated by every rub, how will you be polished?"
-rumi

"faith is the bird that feels the light and sings when the dawn is still dark."
-rabindranath tagore

"your trials did not come to punish you, but to awaken you."
-paramahansa yogananda

Preface

at the height of my life, when everything felt limitless, my partner and i fell gravely ill—suddenly, inexplicably. it was as if we had been cast from eden; one moment, we were falling in love for the first time whilst traveling the world, and the next, we were confined to our beds, our bodies unraveling in ways we could not understand. in the blink of an eye, our worlds turned upside down. we were only 21 years old.

months passed in the shadows of the unknown, each day a test of endurance, where simply making it out of bed felt like a miracle. over time, we were given countless names for the relentless storm raging inside of us: chronic lyme disease, mold toxicity, heavy metal poisoning, chronic viruses, parasites, long-haul covid, hashimoto's, etc.—an endless list.

the past three years of my life have been nothing short of purifying. there were so many moments i wanted to die, moments when the weight of it all felt unbearable. and yet, through the relentless fire of suffering, illusion burns away, stripping back every layer of ego until only truth remain standing amongst the ashes... a truth that inspires me to carry on.

i would never wish this pain upon another, but i do wish
everyone the grace, the compassion, and the depth of
awakening it has given me.

when nothing else could reach me—when doctors had no
answers, when hope felt like a distant memory—Love,
poetry, and the quiet belief in the possibility of healing
became my lifeline. they met me in the darkness, held
space for my grief, and stitched light into my wounds.
they saved my life.

this battle is ongoing, and it is both my greatest
challenge and my greatest gift. it has broken me open,
softened my heart, and strengthened my soul in ways i
never imagined.

more than anything, it has called me to serve—to help
others transmute their suffering into wisdom, their
wounds into healing.

that is the essence of this collection.
that is the heart of *the wounded healer.*

*"there is a reason poets often say, 'poetry saved my life,'
for often the blank page is the only one listening to the
soul's suffering, the only one registering the story*

completely, the only one receiving all softly and without condemnation."

-clarissa pinkola estes

Acknowledgements

to robert, the Love of all of my lifetimes....
you were the steady flame when my world went dark,
the quiet current that carried me back to the peaceful
shore.
the lighthouse that brought me back home to hope again
and again.
no distance, no time, no disease, not even death can
break the thread that binds us.
we will always find our way back.
i love you.

to my mother, who gave up her life so that i may have a
second chance to live mine...
no words could ever reach the depth of my gratitude for
you. only a mother's love could accomplish what you
have done.
i love you.

to my family, friends, and keeva who carried me when i
could not stand, who guided me when i could not see...
your love has been my refuge, your strength my steady
ground. i am endlessly grateful.

to all of the holistic medicine practitioners and advocates

*who are lighting the way to a better, healthier world...
your work is nothing short of divine.*

to everyone who has suffered *from the horrors of
chronic lyme disease or any other illness...
it is not your fault, there is hope for your healing, and
you are a miracle. keep fucking going.
you are never alone.*

and finally, to G*d, Love, Nature, and Art *(whom I
believe are all One)...
you have taught me hat suffering is ultimately a choice
and that the greatest miracle of all is simply to exist. i see
now that there is boundless beauty to be found in the
present moment AS IT IS. i now understand that all
roads lead back to you, even darkness, and that i have
never been (and can never truly be) lost. thank you. all
that i do is in reverence and devotion to you.*

1. suffering into song

once, pain was a weight i could not bear,
a shadow thick, a gasping prayer.
it stole my voice, it stilled my breath
it sang of loss, it hummed of death.

but sorrow, too, can be a muse,
a hollowed heart, a space to use.
for sound and silence, dark and light,
together bring a song to life.

for we are the instrument, G*d is the air,
the light in the void, composing with care,
directing each note, the maestro of Life,
weaving our suffering & joy into music Divine.

what once was ache now takes its flight,
stitched into a harmony of shadow & light.
for even grief, when held for long,
will turn to rhythm —
suffering becoming song.

and all along,
who would have guessed?
darkness reveals the true nature of Light best.

2. eternal now

i want to know
what it is i truly want

what is it that i so passionately desire
the mysterious source that fuels me forward
& ceaselessly thrusts my body into self-perpetuated fire

it keeps me running, always searching for more
blindfolding my eyes, distorting my perceptions
even the beatific vision to it is quite the bore
even the most ineffable moment, imperfection

i thought *perhaps*
the mountains
the seas
the people
the philosophy
the magical mushrooms
wildly chasing my dreams
would satiate this craving
i can't ever quite seem to please

but the void inside only expanded
& swallowed me whole in its ferocious tides

chewed me up into jagged fragments while it laughed &
cried
& spit me out gently
as it contentedly died

hurtling out of the black hole
there was no longer "i"
there was only the sky-less sky & time-less time
desire-less desire & the wind
composing music through the chimes
collapsing every last paradigm
blending all of being seamlessly
into one ever-changing, indivisible
poetic line

how ironic – that what we spend our entire lives
chasing
never required any searching or seeking, running or
craving
it was always the path back to the Present that we were
paving
our very own Heart & Soul we were enslaving

3. open your eyes, sweet seer

open your eyes, sweet seer
do not be afraid to feel it all

fear not the desolate spaces
where the sun's golden rays
cannot reach

do not turn your back
to the places
where shadows seep

for every lovely garden
was once barren land

every painted canvas, once
empty
blank
unplanned

the void of the night sky
choreographs dances
of luminous constellations

can't you see?
in all destruction
lies infinite space for creation

this fear you feel now
is but a wave crashing
into an infinitely abundant ocean

this poem you are reading,
born of pent-up emotion

even in the ferocious rage of forest fire
soil is nourished with nutrients
so that more plants may grow

you, sweet creature
hold within you every ingredient
for the elixir that transmutes
every situation into gold

to reach the mountain peak
we must tirelessly climb
to be entirely gracious of the present
we must first be bound by time

to truly, fully, genuinely understand
what it is to live,

we must eventually die

so, embrace the light
embrace the shadow
embrace every in-between

for rejecting one part
is rejecting the whole, sweet seer

resistance will leave you incomplete...

every fiber, every particle
every last piece of this Universe (& yourSelf)
is your sovereign right to experience

is your Home
is YOU

& is all meant to be seen...

4. the magical mundane

the magical mundane

who tricked you
into tilting your head
up toward the night sky

lusting for far-away galaxies
dreaming of alternate worlds
longingly reaching toward the stars

can't you see?
stars walk the very earth
your feet are planted upon

they make up the very body
through which you interact
with this poetry

they conduct
create
paint
sculpt
this precious moment

as it so happens
they wrote these very words

miracles are the very nature of existence
magic is the essence of the mundane

we dwell inside of eternity
each moment
a moment
we touch "God"

it turns out
finding magic
was never the difficult task
for the magic was never hiding

identifying the "mundane"
as the real imposter
was the challenge
all along

familiarity and complacency
blind us to the beauty
that surrounds us
is us
always

we will continue running infinitely in circles
if we do not soon realize
what is outside of us cannot cure
cannot satiate
our cravings

the "something more"
you so desperately long for
the depth you are seeking
waits for you
not in a different place
not in another person
not in a different set of circumstances
but within your very heart and soul

the entirety of existence dances inside of you

to travel to the furthest edges of the cosmos,
all you must do is journey within

all that you crave
is inside of you
around you
IS you
always

let me know the day

you believe you have met
the mundane

i have found it to be much rarer
much harder to stumble across
than magic

as a matter of fact
i don't know that we have ever been introduced at all

5. the breath of G*d

as i sat there in silence meditating
my awareness concentrated
on each inhale and exhale

i began to wonder ...
is the universe itself the breath of G*d ?

rising and falling into and out of form
unborn and undying
the same energy being recycled eternally

could birth and death simply be different ends
of the same continuum
each depending on the other
to exist
and Life is simply the fleeting glow between

a sigh of light spilling into form, birthing galaxies,
while the inhale draws them back into silence.

what if existence is but a dream
flowing through the mind of the Divine—
a vision cast in waves of time,

where we, for a moment, believe ourselves separate...
forgetting that we are nothing but thought-made-flesh,
stitched from the very same mind
that moves the stars.

what if every heartbeat is a word unspoken,
every moment— the turning of a page
in a book being written and read all at once?
and when we wake from this illusion of time,
will we find we were never apart
from the Dreamer at all?

"oh, yes ... i am meant to be meditating,"
 i remembered

and let go of all theories that begged to control the mystery
for a god defined is a god confined

i blurred back into the present moment
held by the stillness that dwells just beyond the mind

anchored by the familiar pattern of my breath
that guides me Home
to a vast presence
that knows no

such thing as
questions...

6. the weeping willow

the weeping willow

my body is withered & weeping like the willow
where there was once brilliant life, now frail naked
branches
every moment, a battle to hold onto those slippery silver
linings
camouflaged around the all-consuming shadow that is
chronic illness

my mind has fallen dormant like the foreboding winter
it lies crushed beneath layer upon layer of suffocating
snow
blankets of fog denser than stone entrap my comatose
brain
all that i once was disappears into the pitiless
unremitting haze

& nothing of "i" remains

it seems i have no choice other than to bid adieu to you,
identity
it turns out you were never mine after all
so, goodbye body, brain, internal locus of control!

goodbye future plans, expectations, all of those
distractions!
goodbye pastimes, personality, relations!
goodbye to the person i thought i was, and clutched onto
so tightly...

every last dwindling ounce of energy must be rationed &
used solely to survive

so here i lie surrendered, slow as nature
disappearing inside the hourglass
devoured by quicksand & darkness

& as i am unforgivingly tossed about the tempest,
all that endures

is a tender divergence of shadow & light
an impartial stillness
that *somehow* urges me to carry on

for though the illness has stripped me bare,
though every attachment has crumbled into dust,
something deeper remains—
something untouched, unbroken, infinite

a quiet, eternal presence
that has always been here

waiting for me to remember

and so, without anything left to hold onto—
i can finally see what i truly am.

7. the stillness in the eye of the storm

my father and i used to sit on the front porch swing
watching the rain storms roll by,
silently observing the beautiful destruction in awe,
safe from the sky's outburst of emotion.

inside the heart of the bellowing tempest, we dwelt
completely unharmed by its unwavering rage.

we admired the ether's short temper
as she wept of all the worries of the world,
releasing them to the earth in fallen raindrops,
loud roars of thunder,
bright strikes of lightning.

after the gray clouds passed,
the air smelled of rain and earth,
and the world fell silent.

an indescribably familiar feeling of clarity
and peace filled our souls
with calm rhapsody.

oh, how the earth absorbed the tears of the heavens

and alchemized them into an eden of life,
blooming with viridescent shades
and the promise of new beginnings

"i am incomplete without you, pain..."
whispered the universe.

and that is how i learned not to fear sorrow,
but to greet it with open arms and let it guide me —
to witness the tides Life inside and outside of my mind
both rising and receding, *yet always belonging.*

now, i sit in stillness,
watching the storm of Life with Love,
on the quiet porch swing that sways
within my very heart.

8. matter / maya / mother

through the divine mother's womb,
all objects and creation are birthed

transmuted from consciousness into form,
bottomless mystery becomes our physical earth

eternal energy momentarily takes finite shape,
emptiness is given a most-beautiful face

our bodies become vessels for an essence
far beyond our construction of time & space

we are the children of a vast and primary level of reality
a holographic projection of a force words cannot explain

we are the enfolding and unfolding of the seen and
unseen
we are the rising and falling of the wave

the great spirit of life dances through all things
disguised as mountains, valleys, rivers, and seas

matter is the ever-changing face of the mother
love every side of her, and you will see that you have

always been free

the suffering, the drama, the pain, the war
both shadow and light must be consumed

i beg of you, please do not grow weary of this world,
sweet soul
for i am here to tell you ...

*the illusion is G*d, too*

9. will humanity be the honeybee or the locust?

why do we pretend
everything is all alright ?

mass division
pointing fingers
passing the blame

kicking back in recliners like an
entertained audience intendedly observing
as earth burns up in imperishable flame

where did we go wrong ?
have we ever gone right ?

sickness and war and poverty and worshiping money as
if it were god and crime and
corrupt leaders and inequality and mind-dulling
education and working day and night to barely survive
and global warming and destroying earth for "profit" and
overconsumption and increasing health decline
and poison for food and even worse for minds and
instant gratification because we "never have the time"

how can we watch all that's happening
without putting up some kind of fight ?

i fear we've become slaves of our own system
and now only wonder how we plan to commercialize
our very own last act, personally designed:
mass-suicide

can we wake up from our self-induced dream
our delusional righteous psychosis

will humanity be
the honey-bee
or the locust ?

or no-thing at all?

10. O N E / dependent arising

i was taught
life begins at conception
my birthday was december 6th, 2000

i celebrated each year, marking the number
of times i rotated around an object in the sky
with candles delicately placed on a cake

until i learned
i existed as a cell
inside my mother's body
when she existed as a cell
inside her grandmother's body

and that's when i understood
with every fiber of my being
that Life has only ever truly begun once
and since then
it hasn't stopped

from one mother, we all spiral outward
like branches of an infinitely growing tree
one cell dividing, proliferating into many

different petals of the same flower

no distinctions between us
all of the same beginning
the same atoms and energy
arising out of each other

little pieces of the universe exploring itself
molecules momentarily taking shape
manifesting as a unique expression of life
emptiness dancing as all things

the entirety of the universe growing
from one mighty seed

and it's all still happening
from that one place
the only one that exists:
the Eternal Now

where it will happen forevermore

11. (the orange) & the artist

passionately peels
back
 each
 layer
 of
reality

gently puncturing
the surface
& burrowing
beneath
its tough skin

the floor
pulled out
from beneath her
sending her hurtling through the
∞ trap door to eternity ∞

≑ plunging into Life's most-sacred citrus ⇒

roused by its
ELecTriFyInG
scent, made sober by its

i n t o x i c a t i n g
taste, impregnated by its
golden nectar:

⋆ the elixir of existence ⋆

her veins overflowing with
artistic alchemy,
bewitched by creative force—
until all that remains
of the fruit & herself
is but a core,
a stem,
a seed.

the giver & taker
of life & death,
the primary connecting source
between Creator & creation,
the origin & nurturer
of existence itself:
the fountainhead of
consciousness,
awareness,
sentience,
being.

can I squeeze out
one
last
drop, and
s t r e t c h i t o u t
across s p a c e & t i m e
(& a once blank piece of paper)

to fleetingly bridge the g a p,
the ever-growing
c h a s m
Between
language & experience.
...

something as
seemingly mundane as
an orange,
an [aperture]
through which
we can

touch
see
taste
feel
make one

the nature of
EVERYTHING

12. a wild pain

nothing hurts more than being able to see

a wild pain etched lightly into your eyes
from hiding the grief of living deep inside

where a glimmer of hope once used to dance and reside
a flame now flickers, but the ember will not die
a homesickness spreads for a wild freedom that expands
like the sky
a life untethered, unshackled, unbound,
utterly unconfined

for the spirit understands for us when the body cannot
that, someday again, *"volare"*:
we will fly
to a place beyond space,
an hour beyond time

from the wound, rises the soul
who understands the heart's cries
and only listens, and never asks why
because the soul knows, although it hurts,
the pain is what makes us alive

and when i don't know what to say
or how to protect you from the world's lies
and stare blankly at your saddened face as you sigh
because the weight of existence has your hands tied

just know
my pain is holding your pain
through the universes that are
our eyes

and somewhere far away,
but also nearby,
we are watching from above
proud beyond words
of our valiant try
to evolve, to grow, to purify

oh, what a miracle it is
in this Life

to simply get by

13. where i disappear to with you

forever a mystery
it will remain
where i disappear to
some reality far beyond my brain

while i'm in your arms
all that remains
luminescent patterns dancing away
every last lingering remnant of fear
& of pain

free of my body
i am no longer me
floating in heavenly ether
is it all but a dream?

for once i feel entirely lucid in this life
it's almost laughably easy to see
each ounce of unconcealed magic
this strangely beautiful existence breathes

shall we dangle our legs from saturn's rings
or watch those earthly wheels go round & round

shall we laugh or cry or shout or sing
or rest gently in silence: the most wondrous sound

to be free with another; alone, together
the most enchantingly ethereal reverie

all polarity departs, all duality coalesces
all that's left is one inexhaustible energy

sailboats drifting through the sky
the cosmos is our boundless sea
to infinitely explore & create
this playground with you ...

this is my dream of all dreams

.

14. seperation is an illusion

there is a curly-haired boy
asleep on my couch
he rests gently, peacefully
naturally our breath aligns
& with every fiber of my being i feel
we vibrate at the same frequency

trapped behind human bones
suffocated, constricted by a shell
yet so profoundly enabled by sentience
... now how to escape this binding concept of self?

separated only by flesh & thought
division: a convincing illusion
a masterfully induced false reality
"maya": the creator of confusion

for there is no space in - between
me and the being
whom on my couch dreams
& between everything
for that matter —
all i can & cannot see —
more than mirror reflections ...

it's simply all "we"

an omnipotent force
i'll call it : *unity*

we are made of the same ingredients:
atoms & energy, sound & light
no different than the nebulas

we gaze up at in wonder
in our mystically provocative sky

what if
the universe split itself into infinite pieces

to experience every reality, each perspective
to learn about itself in the most accelerated manner...
individuals born of a collective

we have forgotten our intention all along
is to come back to ourself
our center, our home
to uncover the many secrets we behold

it's quite relieving to think
we are the Universe exploring itself

how simple then does that make existence:
we are here solely to live, to experience it all

... all paths become paths of least resistance
no wonder why Love is the most
sought-out experience Here
on this magical earth

for it is us remembering
our initial intention & purpose
recalling why we ventured here first

the Universe finding its way back to itself
the death of polarity self & ego
the rebirth of unity consciousness
where all things are One & equal

...

the curly-haired boy stirs
& abruptly awakes as
i turn the page of my journal
briefly lost between realities
eyes lit up with momentary fear

i wonder if he feels the entirety
of existence itself coursing
through each vein of his body

as he settles like dust
& the fog clears

i smile in his direction
he gracefully returns the reflection

even if we forgot the original game
certainly we are intuitively directed
the objective hardwired in our hearts
the idea melded into our brains, incepted

otherwise the boy with curly hair
wouldn't have every ounce of my affection
or an ironically similar introspection
our love pervades all dimensions
deeper than interconnection
more than mirror reflection

the same spirit divided
riddled by self-subjection

47

...

Love is a lighthouse;
it will always guide us Home.

stronger than all other forces;

it is the universe's backbone

the only reality
the one thing we didn't manufacture

we must retrain our brains not to misperceive it
as an outside attacker

(separation="maya"[illusion])

15. "there is no new thing under the sun"

are we not all poets in disguise?
eternally talking in metaphors
able only to speak almost-truths
teaching through parables
repackaging the same message into different forms
transforming the one magnificent piece of art : Life itself
into infinite unique tangible forms

language enables communication
but there is no way to explain what's unknowable
without reducing it to what's knowable

so, here we will stay
saying the same things in different ways
over and over again
unable to completely capture life's essence
with words that are only shells of all that is
able only to produce blurry outlines
all depth lost in translation

the only way to explain Life
is through comparison analogy allegory

the only way to understand Life
is to cease trying to understand it at all
and instead, to live it...

16. who am i?

i can personally create you a coloring book
traced with the silhouettes of my soul
but any genuine understanding we may have of each
other
dwells some-other-where far beyond shape form &
words
recognized not by knowledge logic observation or
intellect
but by an inner awareness that exists outside
the restricted confines of knowing
past the limits of our *man-who-fractured* reality

i can only sketch for you a hue-less outline
a dim second-hand imprint of who i am
perhaps this poem may help you see
we must not dwell behind these black & white lenses any
longer
because the universe is happening everywhere in-
between
inside a world of gray where the entire color-spectrum
hides

you see –
i am no-thing at all

at least nothing that can be described
a creation being infinitely altered
by something so fluid

6

even art cannot entirely grasp
who is creating who

anyways
i'll meet you outside the lines of the coloring book
& inside of life itself – where there are no limits or
ceilings

bring every color crayon you'd like

17. what do i remember?

i cannot in good faith tell you
i remember anything truly at all
memory itself is a creative act
the feeble human brain at best
stores fuzzy frames
under-exaggerated sentiments
incomplete traces of sensations
or nostalgic fabrications

memory is but a finite shell
encasing the most precious pearl:
the inimitable present

no wonder why
i want to spend every moment with you
i never want to forget that smile

and when i do
how beautiful – that i can dig through every box
inside the cluttered warehouse of my hippocampus
to steal a blurry reconstructed glimpse of it

(p.s your boxes have all of the cobwebs dusted off them.
the constituents lie scattered across the living room floor

in front of the bay window
like old photographs illuminated by the warm wake of
sunlight gleaming in through the blinds.)

18. dance of the wind

as i dissolve into a daydream alongside the still pond
outlined by wild violets & blanketed in lazy lily pads,
my gaze wanders up toward the trees

i study in quiet awe as the wind
choreographs dances for the willow's branches,
luring them from stillness into motion

they sway along to its rhythm,
families of leaves rattling & vibrating
to an irresistible ancient song

i drift into a place somewhere between wakefulness &
sleep
where everything feels like being warmed by a fresh pile
of linens
or being carried to bed by my father as a child, rain
gently falling outside the window

my heart wanders back home to itself

it's in moments like this one, i wonder
if our desire for divinity

is the very roadblock that prevents us from experiencing
it

i think i'll stop searching for something more
give up on answering these never-ending questions
stop chasing after dead ends disguised as shiny thrills

i think i'll let my body be held
by the grassy earth beneath these rotting bones
allow myself to be absorbed into the universe's
somehow-familiar entropy
decompose into this very moment
& surrender to the dance
of the wind

19. creativity is man's highest nature

i watch in absolute awe, completely wordless
as he conjures the sweetest sound
from six little strings
that seems to illuminate the room
in glowing gold light

i watch in absolute awe, completely wordless
as he pulls vibrations from thin air
juxtaposing silence and sound
to create one kaleidoscopic quilt
of heavenly music

i want to wrap myself inside
and drown in the warmth

i watch in absolute awe, completely wordless
as he paints my heart with harmony
choreographing a dance of frequencies
that rise and fall like breath
momentarily existing together as one being

no doubt, an act of divinity
being performed before my very eyes

i watch in absolute awe, completely wordless
as this god in disguise
creates beauty out of pain
alchemizes shadow into light
transmutes the soul of the universe
into yet another beautiful form

i watch in absolute awe, completely wordless
as he looks up at me and nervously smiles
unaware of the sorcery
flowing from his fingertips

... and the entire universe applauds

*(thank G*d ... because no response i could have had
would have ever been enough)*

20. youniverse

*(Universe: 'unified into one, whole' ... from uni- 'one' +
versus 'turned')*

have you ever paused
just for a moment
to wonder if all you see
would still exist
if you were not here
to witness it
into being?

would the sun still burn
its brilliant rays
if they never touched
your precious retinas?

would the mountain
remain solid,
if not for the softness
of your skin?

*is everything not, in some way,
woven in relation to you?*

your eyes—
the decoders of light.
your ears—
the vessels of sound.

you, wondrous being,
call forth the universe,
projecting reality
into existence.

your mind bridges
the microcosm and the macrocosm—
the boundless realm of possibility
and the tangible world of matter.

you, picasso!

your body
super-consciously
self-regulates
without a single command—
your heart beats,
your lungs breathe,
without a word of instruction.

why, then,
couldn't you

perhaps command the tides,
conduct symphonies with the wind,
paint the sky with sunsets?

can you not see
how intricately magnificent
of a creature you are —
a continuum of energy,
a dance of light,
waves and particles
weaving entire worlds of
colors, creatures, music, art—
everything born out of nothing.

how does it feel
to animate the cosmos
as it animates you in return—
to be
the Creator
and the created,
the artist
and the art,
the parts
and the whole,
the particle
and the wave,
the quanta

and the Universe itself...
everything, everywhere, all at once.

you, brilliantly forgetful composer
of existence, playing a divine game
of hide and seek
with yourself.

only the holiest of gods would intentionally forget who
they were
so their power could not corrupt
so their identity could not tempt
so their heart may remain forever pure.

one amnesiac of an artist you are,
one beautiful paradox.

...

(uni - "one; having or consisting of one")
(verse - "writing that is arranged in a rhythmic pattern;
poems")

21. sweet surrender

i know
not one knowing
not one absolute Truth
not one singular unclouded vision

i am not familiar with one lonely story
who has not been skewed

everything i know was created or defined
drilled into the ore of my thinking mind :
constructs labels identities language

every experience & all knowledge
confined within [a limited range of sensory perception]

the human condition is my captor
am uncomfortably familiar with Bias
& quite the stranger to the fair maiden
called Objectivity

... although i believe we were once childhood friends

i can recall a time of gentle innocent being
frolicking freely together hand-in-hand
twirling amongst dreamy fields of wild lilacs
our purple silhouettes laughing under the moonlight

i now
find myself trapped
behind a labyrinth of filtered lenses
a dense jungle of conditioning
a tangled web of domestication
a mountainous mind with thoughts that bellow
like the wind, piercing the Heart
with their frigid bitterness
killing the child inside
ambushing the spirit within

...

i once went searching for answers
only to never return ;
fated to run eternally in circles
always falling short
remaining empty-handed
creating more open-ended questions

somewhere lost inside of infinity
i stumbled across a vial of inexhaustible joy
& delicately placed a drop onto my tongue

its taste was bland, almost nonexistent
its effects unnameable
i suppose we can call them:
surrender

oh how magnificently reality danced
until it rose up into flames
& caved in on itself

i think i saw it smile as it took its last breath

like a fallen phoenix my Heart rose
from the ashes & hurtled my
little lifeless bruised body past
the event horizon

i plummeted face-first
into the unknown

sliding down the rabbit hole
of holographic fractals
i smiled at the mystery, singing:

oh how sweet it is
to surrender

light leaked through the pores of my
skin shattering my flesh &
bones into stardust until
"i"
was no longer

& the scent of lilacs permeated the Universe